# VALENTINES DAY
## COLORING BOOK

by The Coloring Book Art Design Studio

# VALENTINES DAY
## COLORING BOOK

# THIS BOOK
## BELONGS TO

_______________________

_______________________

# LET'S TEST YOUR COLOR

Valentine's Day

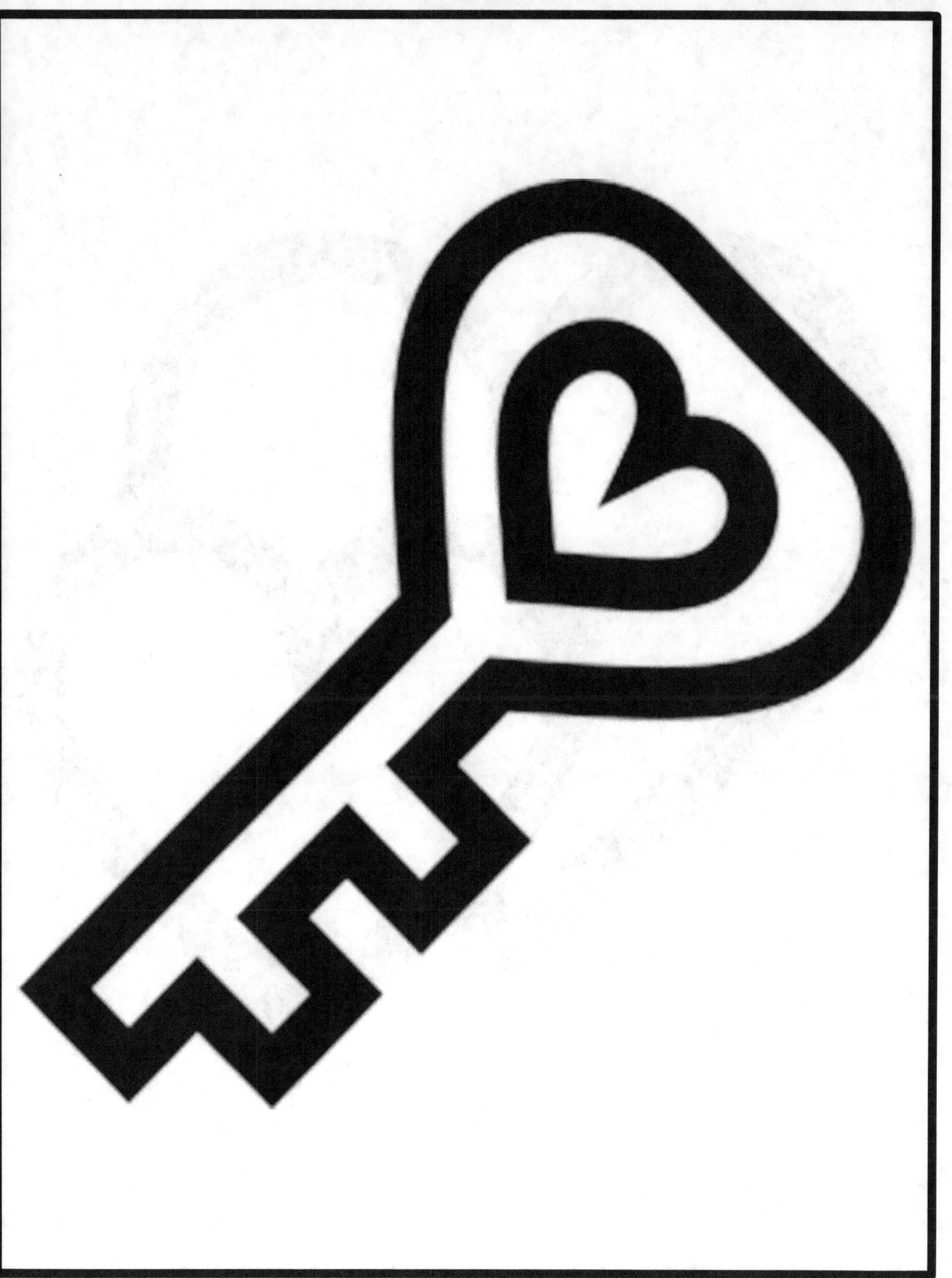

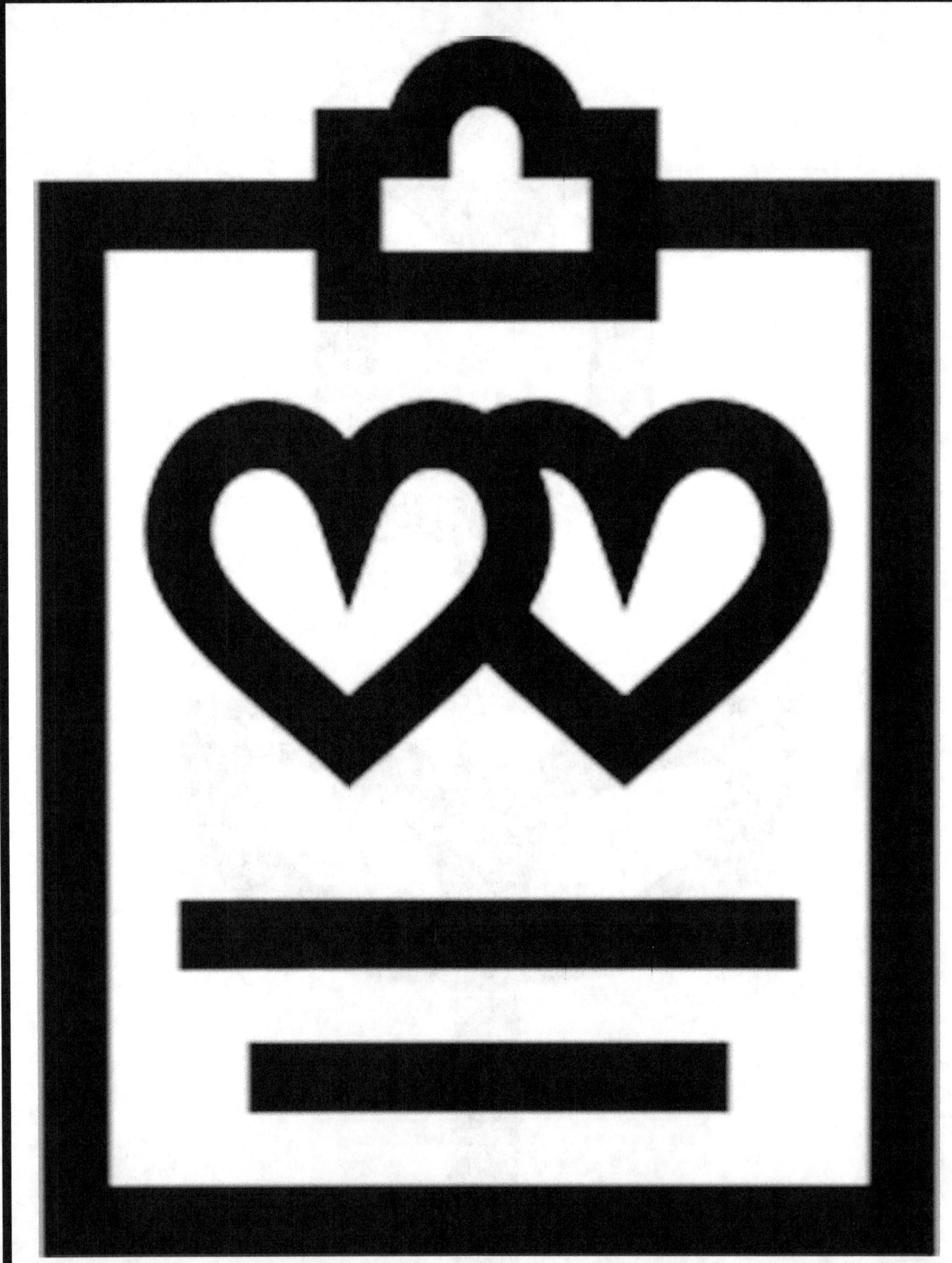

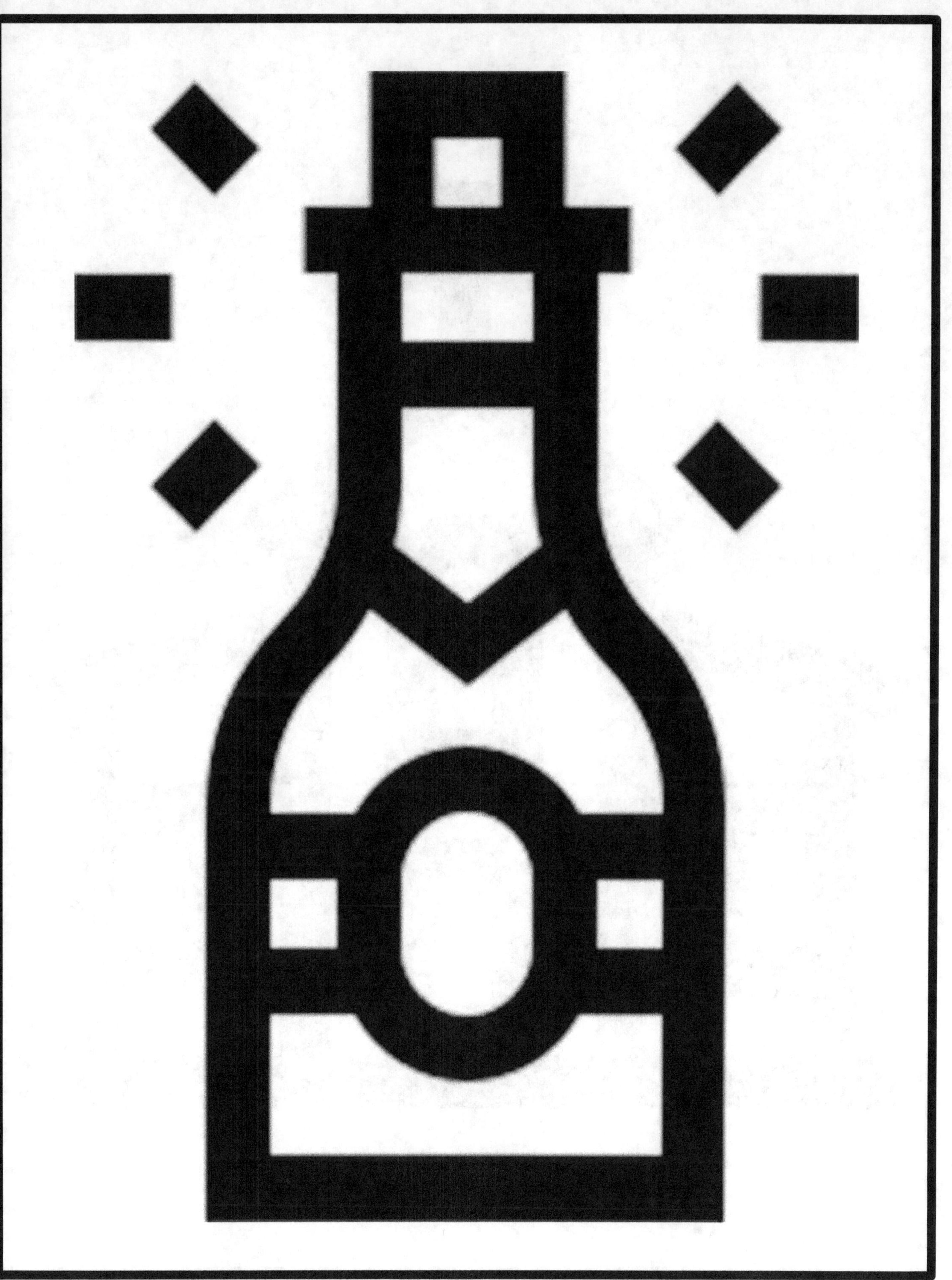

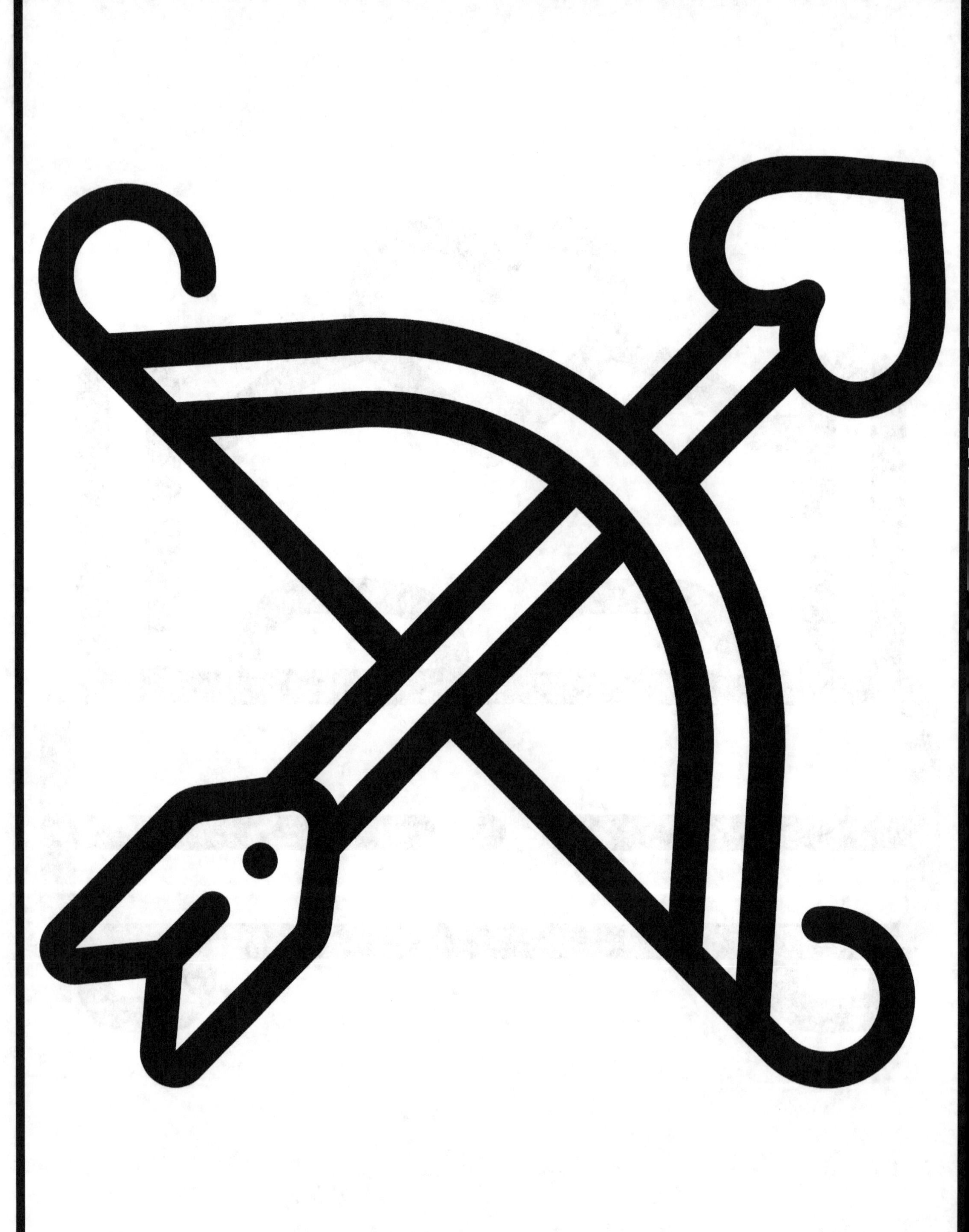

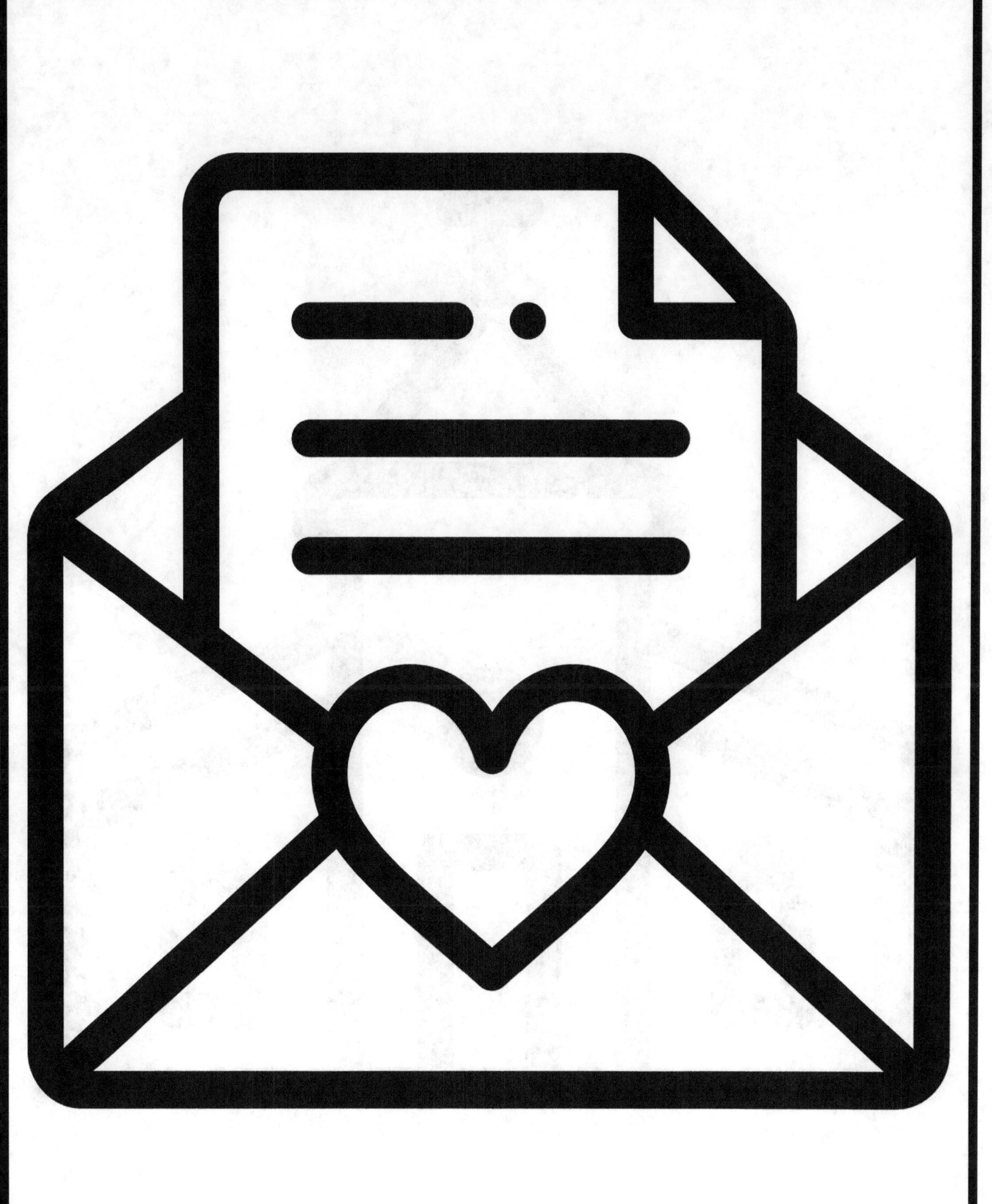

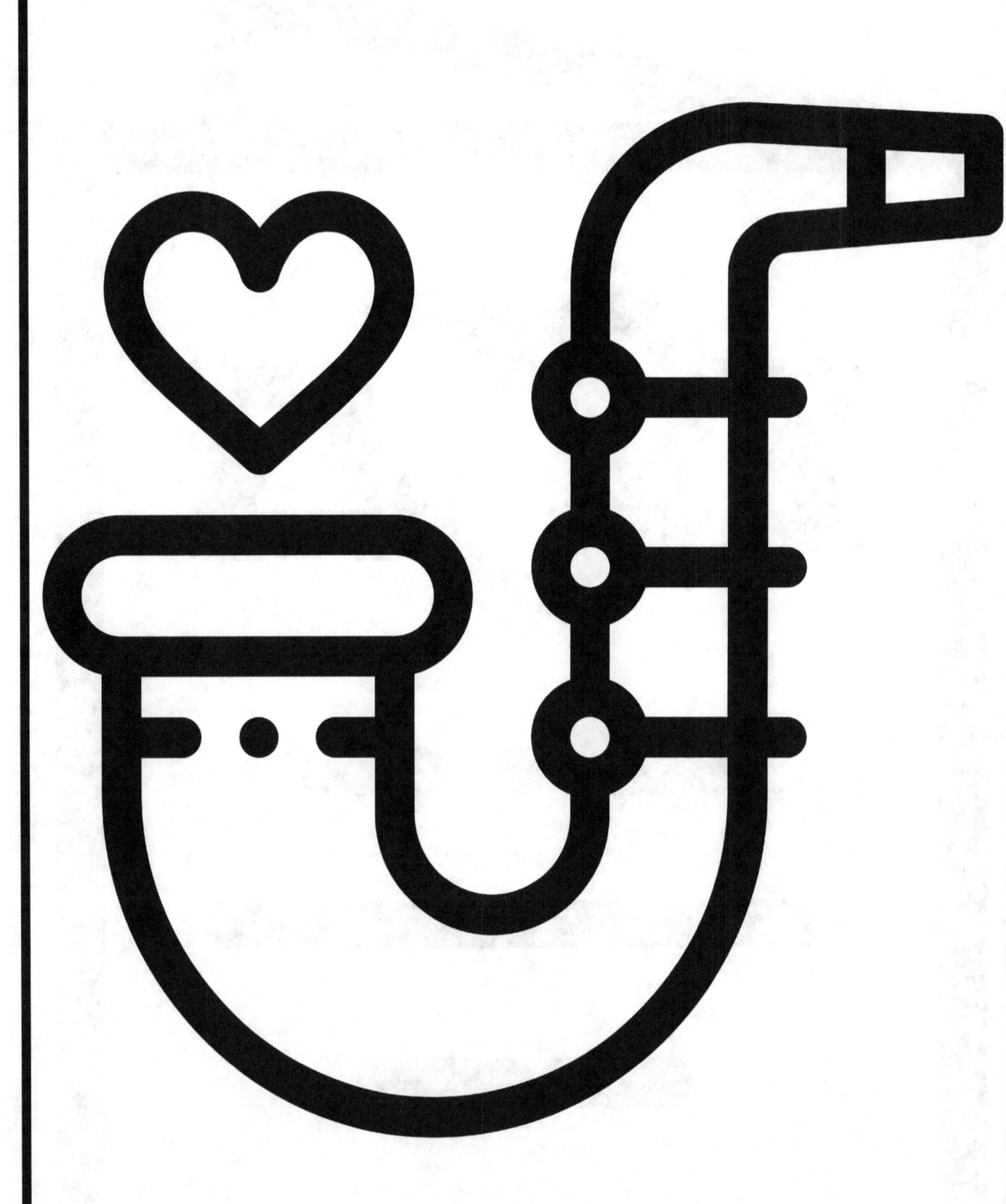

14

HAPPY,
Valentine's
DAY

9 781794 280137